SCHIRMER'S LIBRARY
OF MUSICAL CLASSICS

Vol. 2023

FLORENCE B. PRICE

Sonata in E Minor

For Piano

Edited by
RAE LINDA BROWN

G. SCHIRMER, Inc.

DISTRIBUTED BY

HAL•LEONARD®
CORPORATION
7777 W. BLUEMOUND RD. P.O. BOX 13819 MILWAUKEE, WI 53213

FLORENCE BEATRICE SMITH PRICE (1887–1953) is the first African-American woman composer to achieve national recognition. She was born into one of the most prominent black families in Little Rock, Arkansas. Her father, Dr. James H. Smith, was a very successful dentist, an inventor, and a published author. Price's mother, Florence Irene, from whom she took her first music lessons, was an elementary school teacher and an enterprising businesswoman. Price attended the New England Conservatory of Music, graduating in 1906 after three years of study with a soloist's diploma in organ and a teacher's diploma in piano. There she studied composition with Wallace Goodrich and Frederick Converse and she studied privately with the eminent composer George W. Chadwick, the Director of the Conservatory.

After completing her degree, Price returned south to teach music at the Cotton-Plant Arkadelphia Academy in Cotton Plant, Arkansas (1906), Shorter College in North Little Rock, Arkansas (1907–1910), and Clark University in Atlanta (1910–1912). In 1927, now married and with two children, Florence Price and her family moved to Chicago to escape the racial tension in the south that, by the late '20s, had become intolerable. Here Price established herself as a concert pianist, organist, teacher, and composer.

During the 1920s Price began to win awards for her compositions and her music was published by major publishers including Theodore Presser, Lorenz, G. Schirmer, and Carl Fischer. In 1932 Price attracted the attention of prominent conductors when she won first prize in the Wanamaker Music Compositions Contest for her Symphony in E Minor. The symphony received its premiere in June 1933 with the Chicago Symphony under the baton of Frederick Stock.

Price wrote over 300 compositions, including 20 orchestral works and over 100 art songs and arrangements of spirituals. Her music was in the repertoire of many important ensembles. In addition to the Chicago Symphony, these included the Michigan W.P.A. Symphony Orchestra, the Women's Symphony Orchestra of Chicago, the U.S. Marine Band, and several chamber groups. Still widely performed today, Price's songs were sung by many of the most renowned singers of her day including Marian Anderson, for whom she wrote many of her art songs and spiritual arrangements, Ellabelle Davis, Etta Moten, Todd Duncan, and Blanche Thebom.

A pioneer among women, Florence Price was much celebrated for her achievements in her time. With the resurgence of interest in her music, she is taking her place among those important composers of the 1930s and 1940s, including William Grant Still, William Dawson, and Aaron Copland, who helped to define America's voice in music. Price's music reflects the romantic nationalist style of the period but also the influence of her cultural heritage. Her music demonstrates that an African-American composer could transform received musical forms, yet articulate a unique American and artistic self.

SONATA IN E MINOR

The same year that Price won the Rodman Wanamaker music contest for her Symphony in E Minor, 1932, she also won first prize in the same contest for her Sonata in E Minor. The Sonata is a large-scale, expansive work in the Romantic tradition. The sonata-form first movement (Andante-Allegro) begins with a stately chordal introduction in dotted rhythms. The first theme, in E minor, is a confident and uplifting spiritual-like theme that Price composed. After a short transition, the threefold statement of the lyrical second theme, in C major, follows. Both themes are aptly treated in the development section. The recapitulation leads to a whirlwind of harmonies before the movement is brought to an exuberant close.

The second movement (Andante), a rondo, begins with a lyrical tune reminiscent of the spiritual. It is treated with characteristic syncopated rhythms and simple harmony. The two secondary themes, more classical in orientation, are reminiscent of Chopin and Schumann, respectively.

The third movement (Scherzo-Allegro) provides a virtuosic and rhapsodic close to the Sonata. Technically challenging, the movement is divided into two sections. In the first, the main theme, a descending triplet based on an E minor scale, gives way to a lyrical *cantabile* theme before it returns to close the first half of the movement. The second section is based on a syncopated dance theme. A real "tour de force," the dance theme and its subsidiary themes are taken through a series of meter and tempo changes to bring the movement to a triumphant close.

—RAE LINDA BROWN
UNIVERSITY OF CALIFORNIA, IRVINE

SONATA IN E MINOR

I

Florence B. Price

Allegro

II

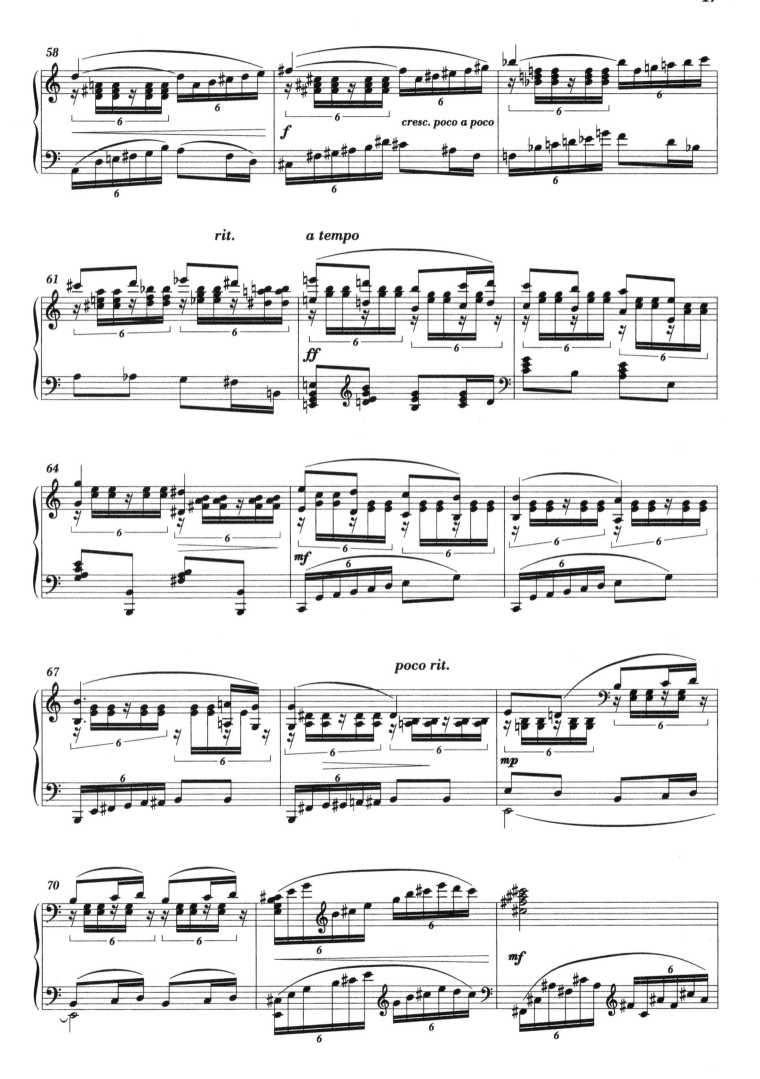

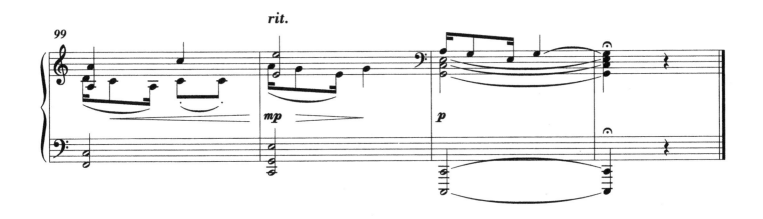

III Scherzo